Overcoming the odds

DR. MARK A MCCONNELL

authorHOUSE®

AuthorHouse™
1663 Liberty Drive
Bloomington, IN 47403
www.authorhouse.com
Phone: 833-262-8899

Published by AuthorHouse 11/27/2024

ISBN: 979-8-8230-3850-8 (sc)
ISBN: 979-8-8230-3849-2 (e)

Library of Congress Control Number: 2024924913

Print information available on the last page.

Foreword

Writing the foreword for my dear friend Dr. Mark Allen McConnell's book, Overcoming the Odds, is a distinct honor and privilege. This work is much more than a simple recounting of events; it is a profoundly moving testimony of resilience, faith, and the relentless pursuit of God's call, even when the journey is filled with trials. Dr. McConnell has lived out the message of this book, and every chapter reveals the depth of his character, the strength of his commitment to Christ, and the unwavering hope that has carried him through the darkest seasons.

Overcoming the Odds invites readers to walk alongside Dr. McConnell as he faces seemingly insurmountable challenges in his ministry. From his first pastorate in Kansas City, where he was called to bring healing to a fractured church, to the difficulties at Prince of Peace Baptist Church in Peoria, Illinois, where division and dysfunction were rampant, he reveals the reality of pastoring in a world that is often hostile to change. Dr. McConnell does not shy away from describing the pain, opposition, and even personal attacks he endured. Instead, he courageously lays bare the vulnerability and weight that come with answering the call to serve.

What stands out most in Dr. McConnell's story is not the intensity of his trials but the tenacity of his faith. Time and again, he turned to Scripture for strength, allowing God's Word to be his guide and comfort. His reliance on verses like Proverbs 3:5-6 and Isaiah 41:10 is a testament to a pastor who not only preaches faith but lives by it. Dr. McConnell's life embodies the truth of James 1:2-4: that trials produce perseverance, and perseverance shapes us into the people God has called us to be. This book serves as a reminder that no calling is without sacrifice, and yet, as Dr. McConnell illustrates, each trial has a purpose in God's greater plan.

Dr. McConnell's story is one of transformation—not only within the congregations he has served but within himself. From his early days at Southside First Baptist Church, through the foundational years at New Cornerstone Baptist Church, to his leadership within the Central Illinois Baptist Association, he has allowed God to refine him and direct his steps. Even as he faced a devastating cancer diagnosis amidst his rise to higher positions of leadership, Dr. McConnell's commitment to God's purpose remained unshaken. Romans 8:28, that all things work together for good to those who love God, has been his assurance, and this book powerfully communicates the reality of that promise.

Overcoming the Odds is not merely a story of survival; it is a testimony of victory through faith. It is an invitation to each reader to embrace their own calling with courage, trusting that God will sustain and strengthen them no matter the obstacles. Dr. McConnell's journey reminds us that God's grace is sufficient, His timing is perfect, and His plans are always higher than our own.

For anyone who has ever felt discouraged, questioned their path, or struggled to see beyond their circumstances, this book offers encouragement and hope. Dr. McConnell's words will resonate with pastors, lay leaders, and anyone who seeks to serve God faithfully, regardless of the cost. He has modeled a life of integrity, love, and unyielding faithfulness. As you read this book, may you be inspired, challenged, and reminded that with God, all things are possible—even overcoming the odds.

In Christ's service,
Claude L. White Jr
Grace Baptist Church, Pastor

Foreword

Mark McConnell knocked the ball out of the park in this book. In it, you will discover many of the challenges every Pastor and parishioner experiences. The blessing in this book is how McConnell shared practical applications to overcoming various encounters in life. Many in the body of Christ are facing tremendous challenges that seems insurmountable, but as McConnell points out, thru fervent prayer and faith in God, you can overcome what appears to be overwhelming. This book is a must-read for all those who desire to win against the odds.

Happy Reading

Pastor Larry Brice
Trinity Love Church
Dallas Texas

CHAPTER 1

Introduction

*A*t *the height of* my pastoral journey, during a season where I felt strong in my calling and deeply connected to my purpose, life took an unexpected turn. I received devastating news: a cancer diagnosis. This came at a time when I was in the midst of running for President of the Baptist General State Convention of Illinois—a role I had been called to with great anticipation and excitement. The news left me dazed, shaken, and deeply unsettled. However, even in that moment of vulnerability, one thing remained steadfast: my faith in God.

In the midst of these trials, I held tightly to the promise found in Romans 8:28: *"And we know that all things work together for good to them that love God, to them who are the called according to his purpose."* I knew that if I nurtured my faith, stayed rooted in prayer, and stood on the unshakable foundation of God's Word, I could overcome any obstacle. My journey was far from over. After treatment, I was declared cancer-free, but shortly thereafter, a new challenge arose.

One year after becoming President of Baptist General State Convention of Illinois, I suffered a significant heart attack. Once again, I found myself facing an unexpected and life-altering obstacle. Yet, through the grace of God, I overcame, continuing to serve faithfully as both pastor and convention president. But as I pressed forward, another challenge awaited me. A year after my heart attack, I lost the function of my kidneys and was placed on dialysis.

In what seemed like a whirlwind of health crises, I found myself confronted with obstacle after obstacle. Yet through every trial, God's hand remained on me. Although I still face dialysis treatments, I am on my way to receiving a kidney transplant, trusting God to bring me through this as He has before.

This book is my opportunity to share what I have experienced and to encourage you, the reader, that no matter what you are facing, you can overcome your obstacles. By trusting in God, nurturing your faith, and maintaining a strong prayer life, you will find the strength to rise above the trials of life. Just as God has brought me through my darkest moments, He is able to do the same for you.

CHAPTER 2

The Call to Serve Amidst Trials

*C*urrently, *I am in* my third, and most likely final, pastorate. My journey in ministry began as a young pastor, only 26 years old, when I accepted my first assignment at Southside First Baptist Church in Kansas City, Missouri. It was a time of great challenge, as the church had recently suffered a significant split. A portion of the congregation had left to start a new ministry, and I found myself stepping into a fractured situation. It was clear to me from the very beginning that my assignment was to love the people of God and to restore order within the congregation. The words of Paul to Titus echoed in my heart: *"For this cause left I thee in Crete, that thou shouldest set in order the things that are wanting, and ordain elders in every city, as I had appointed thee."*

I understood that God had called me to a ministry of reconciliation and order. Just as Paul instructed Titus to establish leadership and maintain good order in Crete, I was tasked with stabilizing this congregation. The task was monumental, and the weight of it often felt overwhelming. But, through prayer and the Word of God, I found the strength to meet the challenge. Every day, I reminded myself of Proverbs 3:5-6: *"Trust in the LORD with all thine heart; and lean not unto thine own understanding. In all thy ways acknowledge him, and he shall direct thy paths."* This scripture became a lifeline for me, a reminder that the work before me was God's and not my own.

My time at Southside First Baptist Church was a season of preparation. I faced resistance and challenges that, at times, made me question whether I was the right person for the job. I remember many nights on my knees, asking God for guidance, and each time, He reminded me of His faithfulness. Isaiah 41:10 was a constant source of comfort: *"Fear thou not; for I am with thee: be not dismayed; for I am thy God: I will strengthen thee; yea, I will help thee; yea, I will uphold thee with the right hand of my righteousness."* God's promise to uphold me was what kept me going. The congregation slowly began to heal, and we saw the fruit of our labor as the church started to grow again. Little did I know that this experience would lay the foundation for future assignments where the trials would only intensify.

After several years of fruitful ministry in Kansas City, God called me to a new assignment: Prince of

Peace Baptist Church in Peoria, Illinois. Like Southside, this congregation had also suffered a division, with a group breaking away to form a new ministry. However, unlike my first pastorate, this time I was called to pastor those who had left. The dynamics were different, but the assignment was familiar: to love the people and set things in order.

At Prince of Peace, I encountered one of the most challenging situations of my pastoral career. Organizationally, the church had deep structural problems, many of which stemmed from a faulty church constitution. This document shifted the authority from the pastor to the deacons and trustees, which led to confusion and dysfunction. Even before I accepted the pastorate, I identified this issue and shared my concerns in a joint board meeting. The deacons and trustees initially agreed to address the problem, but six months into my tenure, they attempted to revert to the old ways.

This experience taught me the importance of steadfastness in leadership. It reminded me of Moses, who had to lead the Israelites through the wilderness despite their constant grumbling and opposition. Just as Moses faced resistance, I, too, had to endure the challenges that came with leading God's people. I found solace in the story of Moses in Exodus 14, where the Israelites, trapped between the Red Sea and the advancing Egyptian army, cried out in fear. Moses responded, *"The LORD shall fight for you, and ye shall hold your peace."* This scripture was a reminder that, despite the opposition I faced, God was fighting on my behalf.

Despite the resistance, God was at work. The church began to experience tremendous growth. Each Sunday, we welcomed 15 to 20 new members into the congregation. Yet, as the church grew, so did the resistance. Some of the leaders were determined to hold onto practices that contradicted the Word of God, and as a result, obstacles arose. The same issues that had led to the original split persisted, and my role was to bring the congregation back to biblical order.

Over the next six years, I faced fierce opposition. Some individuals, resistant to change, tried to undermine my leadership. Things even escalated to the point where some people began to harass my family. They threw eggs at my car, followed my wife, and made obscene gestures toward her. These were dark times, but through it all, I remained committed to loving the people and fulfilling the assignment God had given me. The words of Jesus in John 16:33 became my refuge: *"These things I have spoken unto you, that in me ye might have peace. In the world ye shall have tribulation: but be of good cheer; I have overcome the world."* Jesus' victory over the world gave me the strength to endure.

It was during this time that I truly understood what it meant to walk by faith and not by sight. There were moments when I wanted to give up, when the opposition seemed too great, but God reminded me that the work

He had called me to was greater than the challenges before me. James 1:2-4 became a guiding principle for me: *"My brethren, count it all joy when ye fall into divers temptations; Knowing this, that the trying of your faith worketh patience. But let patience have her perfect work, that ye may be perfect and entire, wanting nothing."* I realized that these trials were shaping me into the leader God wanted me to be.

God's voice guided me clearly during that season. One afternoon, in the midst of the turmoil, He spoke to my spirit and told me to resign as pastor of Prince of Peace Baptist Church—but not to divorce myself from the people. God was leading me to a new chapter, but His love for the congregation remained steadfast. Obedient to His call, I resigned from Prince of Peace and soon after organized New Cornerstone Baptist Church. Again, my assignment was the same: to love the people and set things in order. However, this time, the task was filled with God's abundant grace.

At New Cornerstone, I experienced the blessings of faithful ministry in ways that I could not have imagined. The church flourished, and I was blessed with opportunities to serve in broader capacities. I served two terms as Moderator of the Central Illinois Baptist District Association and two terms as Second Vice President of both the Congress of Christian Education and the parent body of Baptist General State Convention of Illinois. God was positioning me for a higher level of service, and I was humbled by the doors He opened. As Psalm 37:23 says, *"The steps of a good man are ordered by the LORD: and he delighteth in his way."* I saw firsthand how God was ordering my steps, even through the trials.

Just when things seemed to be going well, I encountered a new set of obstacles. In the midst of New Cornerstone's success, my family's well-being, and God's call for me to pursue the presidency of Baptist General State Convention of Illinois, I received devastating news. During my campaign for president, I was diagnosed with cancer. The news shook me to my core, and for a moment, I was dazed, unsure of how I would continue. But through prayer, faith, and the Word of God, I found the strength to move forward. Romans 8:28 reassured me: *"And we know that all things work together for good to them that love God, to them who are the called according to his purpose."* I knew that this was part of God's plan, and I trusted that He would see me through.

By God's grace, I underwent treatment and was declared cancer-free. However, shortly after becoming president of the convention, I faced another trial. I suffered a significant heart attack, which left me weakened and unsure of what the future held. The convention came together in prayer for my recovery, and God heard their prayers. Slowly, I regained my strength and continued to serve both as pastor and as convention president.

This heart attack was one of the most physically and spiritually exhausting moments of my life. I remember lying in the hospital bed, feeling fragile and uncertain. It was a moment when I could have easily given in to fear, but I held onto the Word of God. Isaiah 40:31 became my meditation during that time: *"But they that wait upon the LORD shall renew their strength; they shall mount up with wings as eagles; they shall run, and not be weary; and they shall walk, and not faint."* Even though my body felt weak, I trusted that God would renew my strength.

The convention was an incredible support system during this time. The outpouring of love and prayers from fellow pastors and members strengthened me in ways I cannot fully describe. It reminded me of the importance of community within the body of Christ. Ecclesiastes 4:9-10 says, *"Two are better than one; because they have a good reward for their labour. For if they fall, the one will lift up his fellow: but woe to him that is alone when he falleth; for he hath not another to help him up."* The prayers of others helped lift me up when I could not stand on my own, and I saw the beauty of God's family in action.

Yet, the trials did not end there. A year after my heart attack, I lost the function of my kidneys and was placed on dialysis. Once again, I found myself facing a life-altering challenge. The idea of being dependent on dialysis was overwhelming. It felt like my body was betraying me, and the once strong, vibrant person I knew was slipping away. But through it all, I held onto my faith. I was reminded of the Apostle Paul's words in

2 Corinthians 12:9, where God tells him, *"My grace is sufficient for thee: for my strength is made perfect in weakness."* This scripture carried me through some of my darkest days.

Dialysis became a part of my daily routine, and though it was difficult, it taught me a great deal about dependence—not just on medical treatments, but on God. I learned that even in our weakest moments, God's grace is enough. It was during this time that I began to lean even more heavily on prayer. I realized that while my body might be failing, my spirit could still thrive. Psalm 73:26 says, *"My flesh and my heart faileth: but God is the strength of my heart, and my portion for ever."* This became a cornerstone scripture for me during my time on dialysis.

The physical limitations I experienced also taught me the importance of humility and surrender. In ministry, it's easy to feel as though everything depends on us, but the reality is that God is always in control. Being on dialysis forced me to slow down and allowed me to focus on what really mattered—my relationship with God and my reliance on His strength rather than my own.

Through it all, I continued to serve as pastor of New Cornerstone Baptist Church and president of the Baptist General State Convention of Illinois. Every Sunday, I stood before my congregation, often feeling physically depleted but spiritually energized. I preached with the same conviction, even though there were days when my body felt as though it was falling apart. In those moments, I found comfort in Philippians 4:13: *"I can do all things through Christ which strengtheneth me."* I knew that the strength to continue wasn't coming from me—it was coming from God.

As the months passed, I was placed on the path to receiving a kidney transplant. The hope of a new kidney was a light at the end of a long tunnel. I knew that God's timing was perfect, and I trusted that He would provide at the right moment. Romans 5:3-5 says, *"And not only so, but we glory in tribulations also: knowing that tribulation worketh patience; And patience, experience; and experience, hope: And hope maketh not ashamed; because the love of God is shed abroad in our hearts by the Holy Ghost which is given unto us."* This verse became my source of hope. I knew that God was using my suffering to shape me, and that my hope in Him would never disappoint.

As I reflect on these experiences, I am reminded of the Apostle Paul's words in 2 Timothy 1:9: *"Who hath saved us, and called us with an holy calling, not according to our works, but according to his own purpose and grace, which was given us in Christ Jesus before the world began."* Despite the obstacles, God's call on my life has never wavered. He has been my constant source of strength, and I have learned that even in the midst of trials, we are called to serve. My story is not just about overcoming obstacles; it is about remaining faithful to the assignment God has given, no matter what challenges arise.

Looking back on all that I have faced, I see how God used each trial to mold me into the leader He wanted me to be. I am reminded of Jeremiah 29:11: *"For I know the thoughts that I think toward you, saith the LORD, thoughts of peace, and not of evil, to give you an expected end."* Even when the future seemed uncertain, God's plan was still unfolding. He was using each obstacle to draw me closer to Him, to deepen my faith, and to remind me that His grace is sufficient for every season of life.

This chapter of my life has taught me that God often uses our most difficult moments to shape us for greater service. I encourage you, dear reader, to trust God in the face of your own obstacles. Stay faithful to the call He has placed on your life, and know that His grace is sufficient for every trial you face. Just as He has carried me through cancer, a heart attack, and kidney failure, He will carry you through whatever trials you encounter. You are never alone—God is always with you, guiding you and strengthening you every step of the way.

CHAPTER 3

Facing the Cancer Diagnosis

During the Spring of 2019, I was exuberant and happy. It felt as though God had prepared and positioned me for this very moment—running for President of Baptist General State Convention of Illinois. The sense of purpose and calling was unmistakable, and I began the campaign process with confidence and faith. Through much prayer, I selected a campaign manager and co-campaign manager, and together we started the process of garnering support. The months leading up to this had been a time of great spiritual fulfillment, and I truly believed that God had ordained this season for something bigger than myself.

However, as I began to immerse myself in the campaign, I started noticing a subtle pain in my back and fatigue in my joints. At first, I brushed it off, thinking it was due to the stress of the campaign or the long hours

Dr. Mark A McConnell

spent in preparation. But the pain persisted, gnawing at me, growing in intensity. By the time I visited my nephrologist, I had begun to suspect that something wasn't quite right. After running some blood work, my nephrologist discovered that my Parathyroid hormone levels were unusually high, which had been the case for a while. She suspected the pain was due to a condition called hyperparathyroidism, a disorder that could potentially explain my symptoms.

She ordered a scan of my lower neck to see if one of the parathyroids was over-productive. As I lay in the scanner, I remember praying, asking God for strength, regardless of the outcome. The results came in, but instead of finding an overactive parathyroid, the scan revealed something far more concerning—a lesion on my spine. When the doctor shared this unexpected finding, I felt my heart sink. "This is not what we were looking for," she said, trying to sound reassuring, "but please don't worry. We get negative readings a lot."

Her words didn't quite settle my heart. That night, as I lay in bed next to my wife, I whispered a prayer. The verse from Philippians 4:6-7 came to mind: *"Be careful for nothing; but in every thing by prayer and supplication with thanksgiving let your requests be made known unto God. And the peace of God, which passeth all understanding, shall keep your hearts and minds through Christ Jesus."* I clung to this promise, but deep down, I sensed a storm brewing.

The doctor recommended a bone biopsy to get a clearer understanding of the lesion. I agreed, and the procedure was scheduled at a hospital in Peoria, Illinois. It was a long, nerve-wracking week before the results came back. My phone rang, and my heart raced as I heard my doctor's voice. "The biopsy results came back negative," she said. I felt a momentary sense of relief, but it was short-lived.

Despite the negative result, the doctor remained concerned. She scheduled a second biopsy. However, on the morning of the procedure, the doctor performing the biopsy called me directly. "I don't want to do this," he said. "It feels too risky." He was uncomfortable with proceeding, and his words only deepened my uncertainty. They referred me to the Mayo Clinic, but when my insurance rejected that option, I was directed to Northwestern Hospital in Chicago, Illinois. Another biopsy was scheduled. This time, my wife and I decided to make the trip together. We took the train to Chicago, hoping for the best but bracing ourselves for the unknown.

That night, we spent time exploring the city. Despite the looming procedure, we enjoyed our evening together, trusting that whatever happened next, God was in control. As I lay in bed, I couldn't help but think again of Romans 8:28: *"And we know that all things work together for good to them that love God, to them who are the called according to his purpose."* This verse became a lifeline for me, a reminder that even when we don't understand the twists and turns of life, God is orchestrating something greater.

The third biopsy finally provided an answer—cancer. When I received the phone call from the doctor, informing me of the diagnosis, my world felt like it came to a standstill. I remember sitting in my living room, the phone pressed to my ear, barely able to comprehend the weight of his words. Cancer. It was a word that seemed foreign to my life, my ministry, and my calling. I was in the midst of my campaign to become the President of Baptist General State Convention of Illinois—how could this be happening now? As the doctor's words echoed in my mind, I asked the one question I dreaded most, "How much time do I have?" The doctor paused, and then simply said, "Don't worry about that."

At that moment, a strange and profound peace came over me. The calm I felt wasn't from the doctor's words, but from God's presence. It was as if God was saying, "I have you in the palm of My hand. You will not die because I'm not finished with you yet." Suddenly, the words of Psalm 118:17 sprang into my spirit, *"I shall not die, but live, and declare the works of the Lord."* I clung to that promise. I knew I wasn't finished with what God had called me to do, not for my family, not for my church, and not for the Convention.

The next few days were surreal. I shared the news with my wife, Paris, and we prayed together. Her calm demeanor, her strength, and her unwavering faith in

God were an anchor for me during this storm. She kept saying, "Honey, we will get through this. God is with us." I truly believe God gave her an extra measure of grace to stand firm for me and our family. I had to then face one of the most difficult tasks: telling our three sons.

Our oldest son was 24, our middle son was 22, and our youngest had just graduated from high school and was starting his first year at Northern Illinois University. As their father, I always wanted to shield them from pain and hardship, but I knew I couldn't keep this from them. Each of them took the news in their own way, but one thing was clear: they were there for me. This was a time for our family to grow even stronger, not weaker. I saw it as an opportunity to demonstrate to my sons that life, even in its hardest moments, is never too much for God. This was a lesson in faith, and they were watching how I would respond.

I made a difficult decision. I decided to continue with my campaign for the presidency of Baptist General State Convention of Illinois. Many people would have understood if I had taken a step back, but I couldn't do it. I felt that God had called me to this moment, and I wasn't ready to give up. It wasn't just a campaign anymore—it was a testament to my faith. I knew that continuing to serve as a pastor, to lead, and to campaign while undergoing cancer treatment would be one of the greatest challenges of my life, but I trusted God to carry me through.

As the chemotherapy began, the reality of the battle set in. I started treatment a week after returning home to Peoria, with six rounds scheduled—one every three weeks. The process was grueling, both physically and emotionally. I made the decision to keep the diagnosis private, sharing it only with my immediate family and a few close friends. I didn't want the church or the Convention to know, at least not yet. I wasn't ashamed—I just didn't want to talk about it. I wanted to focus on my duties without the weight of sympathy or concern from everyone around me.

To maintain privacy, I traveled to the next city over for my treatments, ensuring I wouldn't be recognized. Initially, chemotherapy wasn't too difficult. I felt no pain, and I even experienced a boost of energy after each session thanks to a prednisone supplement. For a moment, I thought, Maybe this won't be so bad. But soon after, the side effects hit me hard. My taste buds changed, and food no longer had any appeal. I felt nauseous and drained, and the energy that I once felt quickly left me. My body was no longer my own—it was a battleground, and the fight was fierce.

Then, as if dealing with cancer and chemotherapy wasn't enough, COVID-19 hit. The entire world shut down, including our church. We had to move everything online, and for a time, it felt like everything was falling apart. But even in the midst of the global pandemic, God was still moving. I began live-streaming services from the pulpit each Sunday, and no one, not even my congregation, could tell the changes I was going through. My weight dropped by 20 pounds, my hair fell out, and I lost my beard and eyebrows. But week after week, I continued to preach, and no one knew the physical toll the chemotherapy was taking on me. It reminded me of 2 Corinthians 12:9, *"And he said unto me, My grace is sufficient for thee: for my strength is made perfect in weakness."* In my physical weakness, God's strength shone through.

In addition to my pastoral duties, I organized Zoom prayer calls with other pastors from Baptist General State Convention of Illinois. We used these calls to support each other, particularly during the challenges of COVID-19, but for me, it was also about keeping my campaign alive. These pastors didn't know it, but those calls were as much for me as they were for them. God used those moments of shared prayer and fellowship to sustain me during my darkest hours. The love and support of my fellow pastors were like a balm to my weary soul.

Despite all the struggles, I finished the six rounds of chemotherapy. When I received the results from my PET scan showing that the cancer was gone, I wept with joy. Right there in the doctor's office, I raised my hands in praise. I felt like I had walked through the valley of the shadow of death and was now walking out into the light. The words of Psalm 23:4 rang true in my heart: *"Yea, though I walk through the valley of the shadow of death, I will fear no evil: for thou art with me; thy rod and thy staff they comfort me."*

But the journey wasn't over yet. I went through a brief period of radiation to deal with some lingering pain in my back. The radiation was much harder on me than the chemotherapy had been. It affected my throat, making it difficult to swallow, and I became so sick that I had to be hospitalized for two days to get my electrolytes back in order. Those two days in the hospital were some of the hardest, physically, but they were also a reminder that God was still with me. I clung to Isaiah 40:31, *"But they that wait upon the LORD shall renew their strength; they shall mount up with wings as eagles; they shall run, and not be weary; and they shall walk, and not faint."*

Finally, my treatment was complete. The cancer was gone, and I began to feel like myself again. Slowly, my hair grew back, my strength returned, and my physical appearance began to normalize. The "moon face" I had developed from prednisone began to fade, and my eyebrows started growing back. It was a long journey, but I had overcome. I was not only cancer-free, but I had also won the election for President of Baptist General State Convention of Illinois.

As I look back on that time, I realize that I didn't overcome cancer on my own. It was God's grace, the prayers of my family, my friends, and my church that carried me through. The words of 2 Timothy 4:7 feel particularly meaningful: *"I have fought a good fight, I have finished my course, I have kept the faith."* The cancer was an obstacle, but it was also a part of my journey of faith. God used that time to draw me closer to Him, to strengthen my resolve, and to remind me that nothing—not even cancer—can stand in the way of His plan.

I overcame the odds. I am cancer-free. And through it all, I learned that no matter how difficult the journey, God is always with us, leading us, and guiding us toward His perfect will.

CHAPTER 4

Walking Through the Valley of the Shadow of Death

*I*n *the early spring* of 2022, I found myself fully engaged in supporting my wife, Paris McConnell, as she ran for a school board seat with Peoria School District 150. We spent countless hours together, moving through the community, placing yard signs, attending meetings, and doing everything we could to support her campaign. It was during these moments of regular, everyday activity that I first noticed something wasn't quite right. Each time I bent down to secure a yard sign into the ground, I would find myself short of breath. At first, I brushed it off, thinking it was simply a result of being tired or the stress that comes from a busy schedule. But as the year progressed, these moments of breathlessness became more frequent and concerning.

No matter what I was doing—whether walking, standing, or even doing simple tasks—I would often be left gasping for air. It didn't take much exertion for me to feel winded. The first few times it happened, I paused, caught my breath, and went about my day. I thought it was temporary, something that would pass. I had no idea these symptoms were my body's way of alerting me to something much more serious.

The turning point came in the fall of 2022. I was at home alone one evening while Paris was out of town for work in Collinsville, Illinois. It was a quiet night. I finished up my routine and made my way upstairs to bed. As I reached the top of the stairs, I was suddenly hit with intense chest pain and shortness of breath unlike anything I had experienced before. This wasn't the subtle discomfort I had grown used to—it was sharp, severe, and all-consuming. I knew immediately that this was different. Fear gripped me, and for the first time, I realized that something was terribly wrong.

I stood at the top of the stairs, gasping for air, my chest tight, my left arm and jaw aching. Panic began to set in. Being home alone at that moment made the situation even more terrifying. I was unsure of what to do. Should I call my wife? Should I call an ambulance? I felt my body growing weaker with each passing moment, and a cold sweat broke out on my forehead. I was scared. But I didn't want to worry Paris—she was preparing for a big presentation the next morning, and I didn't want to disrupt her. So instead, I called my oldest son, Moses.

"Dad, you need to get to the hospital now," Moses said urgently. "I'm calling an ambulance."

"No," I insisted. "Don't call an ambulance. I'll drive myself." I didn't want to cause a scene, but looking back, I realize now that it was pride keeping me from asking for help. Somehow, I made it down the stairs and into my car, praying the entire way. My son met me at the hospital, and seeing his face brought me a sense of comfort, but the fear remained.

The emergency room staff acted quickly. After asking me a few questions, they gave me a nitroglycerin tablet, which immediately helped relieve the chest pain and shortness of breath. But as I lay there waiting for the results of my lab work, the reality of the situation began to sink in. When the doctor returned, he didn't mince words. "You're having a heart attack," he said solemnly. It wasn't just any heart attack—it was a significant one. The doctor explained that there was a strong possibility I would need open-heart surgery, but they wouldn't know for sure until they took me back to the cath lab to examine my heart more closely.

At that moment, everything seemed to move in slow motion. I couldn't believe it was happening. I was having a heart attack. My life, my ministry, and everything I held dear flashed before my eyes. I knew it was time to call Paris, no matter how late it was. I turned to Moses and said, "Son, it's time to call your mom." He hesitated for a moment, not wanting to alarm her, but he made the call. It was around 1:00 a.m. when he reached her. Without a second thought, Paris dropped everything, packed her things, and got on the road to come back home. I needed her, and she knew it.

Paris arrived at the hospital just before they were about to take me back for surgery. The doctors explained the procedure to her, but they also warned her that due to the severity of the heart attack, I would likely need to start dialysis after surgery. My kidneys were already struggling, and the dye used during the heart procedure could cause further damage, leading to kidney failure.

But Paris wasn't going to accept that without asking questions. She became my greatest advocate, standing firm in her determination to protect both my heart and my kidneys. "How can you save my husband's heart but put his kidneys at risk?" she asked the doctors. "Can we give his kidneys a day to recover before going through with the procedure on his heart?" She stood there, resolute, advocating for me in a way that only she could. The doctors, though initially reluctant, agreed to delay the procedure for a day to give my kidneys time to recover.

During this time, New Cornerstone Baptist Church went into prayer for me. The congregation, led by faithful prayer warriors, sought God's protection and healing over my life. The pastors of the Baptist General State

Convention of Illinois also organized a Zoom prayer call, and people from all over the state and the country participated, lifting me up in prayer. I could feel the power of those prayers. They provided comfort and strength during what felt like the most vulnerable moment of my life. Psalm 23:4 resonated deeply with me: *"Yea, though I walk through the valley of the shadow of death, I will fear no evil: for thou art with me; thy rod and thy staff they comfort me."* I was walking through that valley, but I wasn't alone. God was with me, and His presence, along with the prayers of His people, sustained me.

After a day and a half, the doctors decided it was time to proceed with the surgery. They took me back to the cath lab, where they discovered that I had one artery that was 95% blocked, another that was 90% blocked, and a third that was 70% blocked. It was a miracle that I was still standing. The doctors had feared I would need open-heart surgery, but by God's grace, the blockages were treated without the need for such an invasive procedure. I overcame the odds once again, and my kidneys, which had been a major concern, recovered. It was nothing short of a miracle.

After the surgery, I returned to my normal life, continuing to serve as the pastor of New Cornerstone Baptist Church and as president of Baptist General State Convention of Illinois. I was grateful for God's hand of protection and healing, but little did I know that another challenge was waiting just around the corner.

One year after the heart attack, I contracted COVID-19 and was hospitalized. COVID took a significant toll on my body, and the virus caused my kidneys to fail. I was placed on dialysis, a life-changing development that I had never expected. But even in this, I saw God's hand at work. Despite being on dialysis, I have continued to serve in ministry. I am still the pastor of New Cornerstone Baptist Church, still the president of Baptist General State Convention of Illinois, and still preaching revivals. Dialysis hasn't stopped or hindered me from fulfilling the calling God has placed on my life. I am overcoming the odds daily, and through it all, I give God the glory.

God has blessed me through my dialysis experience. Every treatment, every challenge has been an opportunity to witness His grace in action. I know that I am well on my way to receiving a kidney transplant, and when that day comes, I will give God all the praise for carrying me through yet another storm. As I reflect on all that I've been through—the Cancer, the heart attack, and now living with dialysis—I can say with confidence that God has never left my side. He has given me the strength to keep moving forward, and for that, I give Him all the honor and glory.

Psalm 118:17 rings true once again: *"I shall not die, but live, and declare the works of the Lord."* Through every trial, I have learned that God is faithful, and no matter what obstacles come my way, He is always with me, leading me through the valley and into victory.

CHAPTER 5

Faith that Overcomes the Impossible

*F*aith is the cornerstone* of my life. It's not just something I talk about on Sundays; it is the very fabric of my being, the guiding force behind every decision I make, and the strength that sustains me in moments of unimaginable trial. My faith in God has been shaped by years of spiritual growth, personal challenges, and the solid foundation laid by my upbringing in the church. From a young age, I learned the power of prayer, the importance of the Word of God, and the unwavering truth that God is always with us, even in our darkest hours.

I grew up in a Christian household, and my wife, Paris, did as well. We were both raised with strong values centered around faith, family, and service. Our journey together has been rooted in our shared belief that God is in control, no matter what life throws at us. That belief was tested when I was diagnosed with cancer. But even in that moment, I never doubted that God would heal me. I stood firmly on the Word of God, refusing to allow fear or uncertainty to dictate my response. Instead, I turned to the scriptures that had carried me through countless other challenges in my life.

One of the scriptures that became particularly meaningful to me during my cancer battle was Isaiah 53:5: *"But he was wounded for our transgressions, he was bruised for our iniquities: the chastisement of our peace was upon him; and with his stripes we are healed."* I held onto that promise with everything in me. I believed that God was not only able to heal me but that He was already working on my behalf. The same God who had called me to ministry was the same God who would bring me through this trial. My faith was strong, and I was determined to continue in my assignments despite the doctor's recommendations to take time off.

When my doctor suggested that I step away from my pastoral duties to focus on my health, I knew that preaching was my medicine. It wasn't that I was trying to be defiant or ignore medical advice; I just knew in my spirit that continuing to preach and serve God was part of my healing process. I had always believed in the power of faith, but this experience deepened that belief in a profound way. Preaching each Sunday became an act of faith in itself, a demonstration of my trust in God's ability to heal me from the inside out.

James 5:15 says, *"And the prayer of faith shall save the sick, and the Lord shall raise him up; and if he have committed sins, they shall be forgiven him."* I knew that as I preached, my spirit was being uplifted, and I trusted that God was working through every message I delivered. Even on the days when I didn't feel strong physically, I was strengthened spiritually. Each sermon became a testimony to God's sustaining power, and I wanted to show the world—my congregation, my family, and anyone watching—that my faith was unshakable. I wasn't just preaching to others; I was preaching to myself, reminding myself of God's promises and standing on His Word.

After I completed my cancer treatments, my faith only grew stronger. I knew that God had brought me through that season for a reason, and I wanted to continue serving Him with everything I had. But just as I was celebrating one victory, another trial came my way. I suffered a significant heart attack. The memory of that night is still vivid in my mind—being home alone, feeling the sharp pain in my chest, and realizing that something was terribly wrong. In that moment, it would have been easy to give in to fear, but instead, I leaned on my faith. I remembered the words of Psalm 23:4: *"Yea, though I walk through the valley of the shadow of death, I will fear no evil: for thou art with me; thy rod and thy staff they comfort me."*

As I rushed to the hospital, I prayed continuously. I asked God to give me strength, not just to survive, but to come out of this experience even stronger in my faith. The heart attack was a wake-up call in many ways, reminding me of how fragile life can be. Yet, even as I lay in that hospital bed, I felt God's presence so strongly. I wasn't afraid of death because I knew that my life was in God's hands. And just as I had done during my cancer battle, I trusted that He would bring me through this, too.

When I was released from the hospital after my heart attack, I preached that very Sunday. Some might have thought it was too soon, that I should have been resting, but I knew in my heart that I needed to stand in that pulpit and proclaim God's goodness. My faith wasn't just something I held in private; it was something I wanted to demonstrate publicly. I wanted to show the world that my trust in God wasn't contingent on my circumstances—it was unwavering, no matter what. Preaching that Sunday was more than just fulfilling an obligation; it was an act of worship, a way for me to declare, "God, I trust You. I trust You with my health, my ministry, my family, and my future."

My wife, Paris, has been by my side every step of the way. Her faith has been a constant source of encouragement for me. She has always believed in the power of prayer and has never wavered in her support for me. Even during the most challenging moments, she would remind me of God's faithfulness and encourage me to keep pressing forward. Her strength and resilience have been a reflection of God's grace in our lives, and I am grateful every day for the partner He gave me.

One of the most challenging aspects of my journey has been the physical changes I experienced due to chemotherapy. I lost my hair, including my beard and eyebrows, and my appearance was altered. But even as my physical appearance changed, my faith remained the same. I continued my responsibilities as pastor and my campaign for President of Baptist General State Convention of Illinois. I knew that my outward appearance was temporary, but my faith in God was eternal. I often thought of 2 Corinthians 4:16: *"For which cause we faint not; but though our outward man perish, yet the inward man is renewed day by day."* This verse reminded me that while my body was going through changes, my spirit was being renewed and strengthened by God's grace.

The weekend after my heart attack, I stood before my congregation once again. I may have looked different, and my body may have felt weaker, but my faith was stronger than ever. I preached with the same conviction, knowing that God had brought me through another valley and that He would continue to carry me through whatever lay ahead. It was during these moments of weakness that I experienced God's strength in a new way. I realized that faith isn't just about believing when things are going well—it's about holding onto that belief when everything around you is falling apart.

When I reflect on my journey—battling cancer, surviving a heart attack, and continuing to lead my church and the state convention—I am reminded of the scripture in Philippians 4:13: *"I can do all things through Christ which strengtheneth me."* This verse has been a source of strength for me throughout my life, but it took on new meaning during these trials. I realized that it wasn't my own strength that was carrying me through; it was Christ's strength. He was the one giving me the endurance to keep going, the courage to keep preaching, and the faith to keep believing.

Faith is not passive—it is active. It is not something we simply hold in our hearts; it is something we live out in our daily lives. My faith was demonstrated every time I stepped into the pulpit, every time I faced another round of chemotherapy, and every time I trusted God's plan, even when I didn't understand it. Faith that overcomes the impossible is faith that endures, that perseveres, and that refuses to give up, no matter what.

After my heart attack, the pastors of the Baptist General State Convention of Illinois organized a Zoom prayer call for me. People throughout the state and across the country participated, lifting me up in prayer. The outpouring of love and support was overwhelming, and it reminded me once again of the power of community. Ecclesiastes 4:9-10 says, *"Two are better than one;*

because they have a good reward for their labour. For if they fall, the one will lift up his fellow: but woe to him that is alone when he falleth; for he hath not another to help him up." The prayers of others helped lift me up when I was weak, and I am forever grateful for the support of my fellow pastors and friends.

After a day and a half of waiting, the doctors finally took me in for surgery. Again they discovered that one of my arteries was 95% blocked, another was 90% blocked, and a third was 70% blocked. Despite the severity of the blockages, I overcame the odds once again. The doctors initially feared that I would need open-heart surgery, but by the grace of God, I didn't. And to everyone's amazement, my kidneys recovered as well. I went on with my life, continuing to preach, lead, and serve.

However, a year after my heart attack, I encountered yet another obstacle. I contracted COVID-19 and was hospitalized. The virus caused my kidneys to fail, and I was placed on dialysis. But even in the face of this new challenge, my faith remained unshaken. God has continued to bless me through my dialysis experience, and I am grateful for His sustaining power. Dialysis has not stopped or hindered me in my ministry. In fact, I believe that God is using this season to strengthen my faith even more. I am still able to serve as pastor of New Cornerstone Baptist Church, continue my responsibilities as state president, and preach revivals across the country.

Every day, I am reminded of God's grace and mercy.

I am reminded that faith is what has sustained me through every challenge, and it will continue to sustain me as I move forward. Even though I am on dialysis, I am overcoming the odds daily. I have learned to trust in God's timing and His plan for my life, knowing that He is working all things for my good. Romans 8:28 has been a guiding scripture for me throughout my journey: *"And we know that all things work together for good to them that love God, to them who are the called according to his purpose."*

There are days when dialysis is challenging, and there are moments when I feel the weight of my physical limitations. But even in those moments, I am reminded of God's faithfulness. He has brought me through so much already, and I know that He will continue to carry me through whatever lies ahead. I am currently on the path to receiving a kidney transplant, and I trust that in His perfect timing, God will provide. I believe that just as He has done before, God will bring me through this season as well.

One of the most powerful lessons I have learned through these trials is the importance of perseverance. The Apostle Paul writes in 2 Corinthians 4:8-9, *"We are troubled on every side, yet not distressed; we are perplexed, but not in despair; Persecuted, but not forsaken; cast down, but not destroyed."* These words have resonated with me deeply as I have faced one challenge after another. Life has pressed me on every side, but I have not been crushed. I have faced moments of despair, but I have never lost hope because I know that God is with me.

Faith is not just about overcoming physical challenges; it is about overcoming the mental and emotional battles that come with them. There were times during my journey when doubt tried to creep in, when I questioned why I was facing so many obstacles. But each time, I turned to the Word of God for comfort and reassurance. Psalm 46:1 says, *"God is our refuge and strength, a very present help in trouble."* In those moments of doubt, I reminded myself that God was my refuge and strength. I found peace in knowing that He was always present, even in the midst of my trouble.

My faith was also strengthened by the prayers and support of my church family at New Cornerstone Baptist Church. They went into fervent prayer for me during every trial I faced. The power of their prayers, combined with my own faith, created a fortress around me. I knew that I was not walking through these challenges alone. My church stood with me, prayed for me, and believed with me that I would come out victorious. I am incredibly blessed to have such a loving and supportive congregation, and their faith in God's healing power fueled my own.

The journey has not been easy, but it has been filled with moments of grace and mercy. I have seen firsthand how God can take the most difficult circumstances and use them for His glory. As I continued to serve as the pastor of New Cornerstone and as President of the Baptist General State Convention of Illinois, I witnessed God's hand at work in my life and in the lives of those around me. My testimony of overcoming cancer, surviving a heart attack, and continuing to serve while on dialysis has inspired others to trust in God's power. People have shared with me how my journey has encouraged them to hold onto their faith in the midst of their own trials.

One of the most profound moments of this journey occurred when I stood in the pulpit, just days after being released from the hospital following my heart attack. My body was weak, but my spirit was strong. I preached that Sunday morning with a renewed sense of purpose, knowing that God had given me another chance to proclaim His Word. I could feel His strength flowing through me, and I realized that faith is not about avoiding trials, but about enduring them with grace and trust in God's plan.

My wife, Paris, has been my greatest supporter throughout this entire journey. Her faith has been a rock for me, and her encouragement has given me the strength to keep going when I felt like giving up. She has walked with me through every doctor's appointment, every hospital stay, and every moment of uncertainty. Together, we have prayed, wept, and celebrated God's faithfulness. Our marriage has been strengthened by these trials, and I am grateful for the partner God gave me to walk through life with.

Faith that overcomes the impossible is not passive—it requires action. It requires standing on the Word of God, even when everything around you is falling apart. It requires trusting in His promises, even when the future seems uncertain. It requires continuing to serve, even when your body is weak and your strength is failing. And most of all, it requires believing that God is good, no matter what.

As I look ahead to the future, I know that more challenges may come my way. But I am not afraid. I have seen what God can do. I have experienced His healing power, His provision, and His grace. My faith has been tested, but it has also been strengthened. I am walking by faith, knowing that God is with me every step of the way.

The road to my kidney transplant is a journey of faith in itself. Each day, as I wait for the call that will change my life, I trust in God's perfect timing. I know that He has already written the story of my life, and that every chapter is part of His greater plan. Isaiah 40:31 has been a constant reminder of God's promise: *"But they that wait upon the LORD shall renew their strength; they shall mount up with wings as eagles; they shall run, and not be weary; and they shall walk, and not faint."* I believe that God will renew my strength, and that I will continue to soar, run, and walk in His grace.

Faith has carried me through every trial, and it will continue to carry me through whatever lies ahead. I give God all the praise for the journey He has brought me through, and I am confident that the best is yet to come. As I stand in the pulpit each Sunday, as I lead my congregation, and as I serve Baptist General State Convention of Illinois, I do so with a heart full of gratitude and a faith that has been tested and proven strong.

In the end, it is not about the obstacles we face, but about the God who helps us overcome them. My faith has brought me through the impossible, and I know that it will continue to bring me through whatever comes next. I stand as a testimony to God's faithfulness, and I will continue to proclaim His goodness for as long as I have breath.

I give God all the glory, for He has truly done the impossible in my life. And I know that He can do the same for anyone who trusts in Him. Faith that overcomes the impossible is available to all who believe. Keep the faith, and watch God move mountains in your life, just as He has done in mine.

CHAPTER 6
Encouraging Others to Hold On

I *share my experiences* to encourage others because we all go through something. We all encounter obstacles, but thank God we can overcome the odds. Regardless of what you go through, you can make it. If I can leave anything with those who hear my story, it's this: Don't ever lose hope. God is with us through every trial, and He strengthens us to face what seems impossible. One of the things that gave me strength during my journey was knowing that my testimony could inspire others who were also walking through their own valleys.

I remember during my cancer treatment, I had been invited to preach a revival in Michigan. To most people, it would have seemed like the last thing I should be doing—traveling, preaching, and exerting energy while my body was fighting cancer. But to me, it was a reminder that even in the midst of our trials, God can still use us.

My spirit was willing, and though my body was weak, I believed that God had given me the strength to do what He had called me to do. Preaching wasn't just my job, it was my lifeline. It was how I stayed connected to my purpose, and it was how I showed God—and myself— that I trusted Him completely.

I remember standing in that pulpit, my body worn from chemotherapy, but my heart full of faith. I told the congregation, "I am not here because I feel great physically. I am here because my God is great, and I trust Him with everything." The people responded with such love and compassion, but more than that, they were encouraged. You see, they saw someone who wasn't allowing their circumstances to dictate their faith. They saw someone who was choosing to serve God, even in the midst of suffering. And I think that's what spoke to them more than any words I could have preached.

We all need that encouragement sometimes. We need to see that it's possible to keep going, even when the road gets tough. That's why I share my testimony. It's not to highlight my strength, but to highlight God's strength working through me. It's to show others that even when life takes unexpected turns, we can trust God to carry us through.

When I look back at my life, I realize that every trial I've faced has been an opportunity to encourage others. Whether it was my battle with cancer, my heart attack, or even my journey with dialysis, each obstacle was a chance to say to someone else, "If God brought me through this, He can bring you through your situation too."

Sometimes, encouragement comes in the form of simply being present. I've often visited people in hospitals, and I don't always have the right words to say. But I've learned that it's not always about what you say—it's about showing up. It's about letting people know that they are not alone, and that someone else has walked through the fire and come out on the other side. The Bible says in 2 Corinthians 1:3-4, *"Blessed be God, even the Father of our Lord Jesus Christ, the Father of mercies, and the God of all comfort; Who comforteth us in all our tribulation, that we may be able to comfort them which are in any trouble, by the comfort wherewith we ourselves are comforted of God."* That scripture is a powerful reminder of why it's so important to encourage others. When God comforts us in our time of need, He equips us to comfort others in theirs.

During my time on dialysis, I encountered many people who were discouraged. They were dealing with their own health struggles and facing an uncertain future. I remember speaking to one man who had been on dialysis for years. He was tired, worn out, and questioning whether he could keep going. I shared my story with him, how I had faced cancer and a heart attack, and how I was now on dialysis, but still serving as a pastor and state convention president. I told him that even though it was hard, God was still good. I reminded him that God had a plan for his life, and that he wasn't forgotten. By the end of our conversation, he was smiling. He told me, "I needed to hear that today." That's what it's all about—being able to lift someone's spirit when they're feeling low.

I believe that one of the greatest gifts we can give to others is the gift of hope. Hope is powerful because it points us beyond our current circumstances and reminds us that there's something greater ahead. The Bible says in Romans 5:3-5, *"And not only so, but we glory in tribulations also: knowing that tribulation worketh patience; And patience, experience; and experience, hope: And hope maketh not ashamed; because the love of God is shed abroad in our hearts by the Holy Ghost which is given unto us."* That scripture has been a constant source of strength for me. It reminds me that even in the middle of our sufferings, God is building something in us—patience, experience, and most importantly, hope.

I encourage anyone reading this to hold on to hope, no matter what you're facing. It may feel like you're in the darkest part of your life right now, but God is with you. He's working in ways you can't see, and He's preparing you for something greater. One of the things that has helped me in my darkest moments is remembering that God's plans are bigger than mine. Isaiah 55:8-9 says, *"For my thoughts are not your thoughts, neither are your ways my ways, saith the Lord. For as the heavens are higher than the earth, so are my ways higher than your ways, and my thoughts than your thoughts."* We may not always understand why we go through certain trials, but we can trust that God is in control and that His ways are higher than ours.

Another key to holding on during difficult times is staying connected to your faith community. Whether it's your church, a small group, or even just a few close friends, having people around you who can pray for you, support you, and encourage you is crucial. I'm so grateful for the pastors and members of the Baptist General State Convention of Illinois who prayed for me during my health struggles. They organized prayer calls, checked in on me, and lifted me up when I was feeling weak. I know that their prayers made a difference in my life, and I encourage you to lean on your faith community when you're going through tough times.

Encouraging others also means being vulnerable about your own journey. Sometimes we think that we have to have everything together in order to help someone else, but the truth is, people are often encouraged by our honesty. When we share our struggles and how God brought us through, it gives them permission to be honest about their own struggles. It shows them that it's okay to not have all the answers, and that God is with us even when we feel lost or confused.

I've learned that people aren't looking for perfection—they're looking for authenticity. They want to know that the person encouraging them has been through something, too, and that they're not alone in their journey. That's why I'm always open about my experiences with cancer, heart disease, and dialysis. I want others to know that while I've faced some tough battles, God has been faithful through them all.

As I continue on my own journey, I'm committed to encouraging others to hold on to their faith. I believe that God uses each of us to be a light to someone else, and I pray that my story will inspire others to keep trusting in God, no matter what they're facing. Life is full of ups and downs, but through it all, God is good. He is our source of strength, our hope, and our comfort. And just as He has brought me through the storms of life, He will bring you through, too.

So, hold on. Keep the faith. Don't give up. God is with you, and He is working all things together for your good. You may not see the full picture yet, but trust that God's plan for your life is good, and He will carry you through whatever challenges you face. As Psalm 27:14 says, *"Wait on the Lord: be of good courage, and he shall strengthen thine heart: wait, I say, on the Lord."* Waiting on God can be hard, especially when we're in the middle of a storm, but I've learned that His timing is perfect, and His ways are always best.

As you continue on your journey, I pray that you will find strength in God's promises, hope in His Word, and peace in His presence. And when you come out on the other side of your trial, I encourage you to share your story with others, so that they, too, can be encouraged to hold on and keep the faith.

CHAPTER 7

By My Side: The Strength of a Loving Spouse

*T*here are three words that encapsulate the incredible strength and support I received from my wife during some of the most challenging moments of my life: Support, Encouragement, and Advocate. Each of these words embodies the essence of who she was to me as I faced daunting obstacles, including my cancer diagnosis, heart attack, and loss of kidney function. This chapter is an exploration of how Paris, my loving wife, became the anchor that held me steady through the storm.

Support: The Foundation of Resilience

From the moment we exchanged vows, Paris has been more than a life partner—she has been my steadfast supporter. This role became especially pronounced during the most turbulent seasons of my life. When the diagnosis of cancer came with the weight of fear and uncertainty, Paris was the first to rise to the occasion. She organized medical appointments, researched treatment options, and stood by my side during consultations, listening intently and asking thoughtful questions to ensure I had the best care possible. Her presence alone was a balm, soothing the silent anxieties that often threatened to overwhelm me.

I remember one instance vividly when the fatigue from chemotherapy took a toll on me, both physically and emotionally. I found myself questioning if I could continue preaching, fulfilling pastoral duties, and pursuing the presidency of the Baptist General State Convention of Illinois. Paris would sit next to me during those quiet moments, holding my hand, looking into my eyes, and speaking words that were simple yet powerful: "You are not alone in this." Those words renewed my strength and reminded me that I had a partner who believed in me, even when my body and spirit felt depleted.

She also took on more responsibilities around the house without a word of complaint. From handling the logistics of our daily lives to managing family needs, her seamless balance of these tasks allowed me to focus on healing and maintaining my ministry work. Her dedication to supporting me was not just in the big moments but also in the countless small ones that often go unnoticed—bringing a glass of water during a restless night, reminding me of medication schedules, or sharing a smile when words felt heavy.

Encouragement: Breathing Life into Hope

Encouragement is a powerful force that can light up the darkest paths, and Paris wielded it like a masterful artisan. The challenges we faced were not merely physical; they were spiritual and emotional as well. My wife knew that, beyond my body, my spirit also needed nurturing. She would remind me of God's promises, quoting scriptures like Isaiah 41:10: *"Fear thou not; for I am with thee: be not dismayed; for I am thy God: I will strengthen thee; yea, I will help thee; yea, I will uphold thee with the right hand of my righteousness."* Hearing these words from her, a voice so familiar and full of love, made the scripture come alive in new ways. They weren't just verses; they were declarations of faith she spoke over me.

Paris's encouragement was constant but never forced. She understood the balance between allowing me to process my emotions and gently steering me back to hope when despair loomed. On days when I felt particularly burdened, she would share stories of people who had overcome similar trials and point out the miracles, big and small, that surrounded us daily. Whether it was a phone call from a friend, an unexpected good day amidst treatment, or the simple blessing of being together, Paris made sure we saw the moments of light that were too easy to overlook.

Her voice of encouragement was also present in moments when I continued my pastoral duties. Paris watched me preach on Zoom and helped me set up my space to ensure I looked and felt my best despite the fatigue. Before every virtual service, she would look at me with that confident smile of hers and say, "God's message is in you, and He will carry you through." This unwavering belief in my calling gave me the push I needed to keep moving forward, even on days when my body resisted.

Advocate: Championing My Journey

Perhaps one of the most significant roles Paris played was that of an advocate. She not only advocated for my medical needs but also for my emotional and spiritual well-being. In hospital rooms and doctors' offices, she was my voice when I struggled to find my own. She asked questions I didn't think to ask, pushed for clarity when answers seemed vague, and made sure that I received the attention and care I needed.

Paris's advocacy extended beyond the clinical environment. She shielded me from unnecessary stressors and protected our space so that I could rest and recharge. Family members and friends often wanted updates, and while they were well-meaning, their inquiries could be overwhelming. Paris managed communications, providing updates and fielding questions so that I could focus on healing without the weight of explaining my journey repeatedly.

Her advocacy also had a deeply personal side. Paris knew when I needed solitude and when I needed company. She became adept at reading my silent cues, understanding that true advocacy wasn't just about speaking up for someone but knowing when to be their quiet companion. During moments when words failed me, Paris would simply sit by my side, her presence a testament that I was seen and loved.

Even beyond the immediate challenges of cancer and health issues, Paris's advocacy showed itself when I resumed my duties and ultimately pursued the presidency of the State Convention. There were times when my health was questioned by those who didn't know the extent of what I was enduring. Paris stood firm, reinforcing that my capabilities should not be underestimated despite the trials I was facing. Her faith in my strength and God's plan for us empowered me to move forward with confidence, even in the face of doubt from others.

The Unseen Battles

What many people didn't realize is that Paris was fighting battles of her own. Supporting a spouse through illness is no easy task, and it takes a toll emotionally and physically. Yet, she remained strong, even in her most vulnerable moments. There were nights when I would catch a glimpse of her quiet tears—moments she didn't intend for me to see. They were tears of concern, exhaustion, and love. It was in those moments that I truly understood the depth of her strength; she allowed herself to feel the weight of our situation but never let it hinder her role as my support system.

Paris's journey was marked by sacrifice, resilience, and an unyielding commitment to stand by my side. Her love and strength were woven into every stage of my recovery, making her an integral part of my story. The impact she had on my ability to overcome cannot be overstated. I not only survived those difficult seasons but thrived, in large part, because of her.

A Testament to Love

The bond between us deepened through each trial, turning moments of difficulty into memories of shared victory. Our love story became one not just of joy and partnership, but of endurance and grace. Paris's support, encouragement, and advocacy were more than acts of love; they were lifelines that carried me through. Her faith mirrored and strengthened mine, reminding me that the journey was not just mine alone to bear.

To this day, the gratitude I have for her unwavering presence is immeasurable. Through support, encouragement, and advocacy, Paris showed me that love, in its purest form, has the power to transform suffering into hope and trials into triumphs.

CHAPTER 8

Rejoicing After the Battle

W hen my oncologist told me I was cancer-free, I could hardly contain my joy. Right there in her office, I began rejoicing and praising God. I didn't care who saw me; I didn't care how loud I was. At that moment, I was overwhelmed with gratitude. God had brought me through the valley of cancer, and I knew without a doubt that it was His hand that had healed me. I had prayed, trusted, and held on to my faith, and now I was standing on the other side of the storm, victorious. There is something powerful about giving God praise in the moment of triumph. It's a testimony to His goodness and faithfulness.

After hearing the words "cancer-free," I immediately thought back to the moments when I didn't know how the journey would end. I remembered the days of chemotherapy when I felt weak, sick, and unsure of what was ahead. I remembered the prayers I prayed when fear tried to creep in, and the promises of God that I clung to in the darkest moments. And now, standing on the other side, my heart couldn't help but burst with gratitude. I knew that my healing wasn't just for me—it was a testimony to others, to show them what God can do when we trust Him through the battle.

When I left the oncologist's office and went home to share the news with my wife, Paris, and our children, the rejoicing continued. As a family, we had walked through this battle together, and now we could celebrate together. God had been faithful, not only to me but to all of us. My wife, who had prayed for me, cared for me, and encouraged me every step of the way, stood by my side, and we praised God together. There is a special kind of joy that comes when you've been through the fire and come out on the other side, still standing. And that's exactly what we did—we stood and praised God for His faithfulness.

But it wasn't just after my cancer battle that I rejoiced. After I recovered from my heart attack, I found myself once again giving God all the glory. I remember coming home from the hospital, feeling weak but grateful. I knew that I had faced death head-on, but God had spared me once again. When I got home, I dropped to my knees and thanked Him for allowing me to see another day, for giving me more time with my family, my church, and the people I serve.

Recovering from the heart attack was another journey of faith. There were moments when I wondered how long it would take to regain my strength, but I trusted that God was still with me. Each day, as I got stronger, I was reminded of His sustaining power. And when I was finally able to return to the pulpit, I couldn't help but lift my hands and give Him praise in front of the congregation. I told them, "God has been good to me. He has kept me through the battle, and for that, I will give Him all the glory." There is something about worshiping God after the storm has passed—it feels like a victory dance, a celebration of His power and His presence.

As believers, we often talk about praising God in the storm, and that's important. But we must also remember to praise Him after the storm, when the battle is over, and we've come through to the other side. That's when our testimony is the strongest. That's when others can see that our God is not only a God who walks with us through the valley, but a God who leads us out of it with victory in our hands.

For me, each battle—whether it was cancer, a heart attack, or even my current journey with dialysis—has been an opportunity to deepen my faith. But each victory has also been an opportunity to rejoice, to shout from the rooftops that God is faithful. He is Jehovah Rapha, the Lord who heals. He is Jehovah Jireh, the Lord who provides. And He is Jehovah Nissi, the Lord our banner, who goes before us in every battle.

The Bible is full of examples of people who rejoiced after their battles. One of my favorites is King David, who often praised God after experiencing great deliverance. In Psalm 18:1-2, David says, *"I will love thee, O Lord, my strength. The Lord is my rock, and my fortress, and my deliverer; my God, my strength, in whom I will trust; my buckler, and the horn of my salvation, and my high tower."* David knew what it was like to face battles, but he also knew the power of rejoicing after the victory. His psalms are full of praise to God for His faithfulness, and they remind us that no matter how fierce the battle, God is our deliverer.

When I think about my own journey, I can't help but be reminded of the Israelites crossing the Red Sea. They had been in bondage for so long, but God delivered them in a mighty way. When they crossed over to the other side, they sang a song of praise to the Lord. In Exodus 15:1-2, it says, *"Then sang Moses and the children of Israel this song unto the Lord, and spake, saying, I will sing unto the Lord, for he hath triumphed gloriously: the horse and his rider hath he thrown into the sea. The Lord is my strength and song, and he is become my salvation: he is my God, and I will prepare him an habitation; my father's God, and I will exalt him."*

That's what we must do after every battle—sing a song of praise to the Lord. We must remember that it was God who brought us through, and we must never stop giving Him the glory. The same God who parted the Red

Sea is the same God who heals, restores, and strengthens us today. And just as the Israelites rejoiced after their deliverance, we too must rejoice after our battles.

Looking back, I realize that every battle has been a stepping stone to greater faith. Each time I faced a challenge, God was teaching me something new about His character, His faithfulness, and His power. And each time I came out on the other side, my faith was stronger. I rejoiced not just because I was healed or restored, but because I had seen God's hand at work in my life in a new way. And that is worth celebrating.

So, as I continue on this journey, I make it a point to rejoice after every battle. I make it a point to give God the glory, to share my testimony, and to remind others that no matter what they are facing, God is able to bring them through. There is power in rejoicing after the battle because it shifts our focus from what we went through to who brought us through it. It reminds us that we serve a mighty God, and it strengthens our faith for the battles yet to come.

One of the reasons I believe in the power of rejoicing is because it is a form of spiritual warfare. When we praise God, even after the battle is over, we are declaring that the enemy did not win. We are saying that despite everything we went through, we are still standing, and our faith is stronger than ever. The devil wants to keep us focused on the pain, the suffering, and the hardship, but when we praise God, we shift our focus to His goodness, His power, and His victory in our lives.

I've learned that rejoicing after the battle is not just about celebrating the fact that the storm is over—it's about celebrating the fact that God is still in control. It's about acknowledging that even when we didn't understand what was happening, God was working behind the scenes, orchestrating everything for our good. Romans 8:28 says, *"And we know that all things work together for good to them that love God, to them who are the called according to his purpose."* That's the kind of God we serve—a God who can take the worst situations and turn them around for our good.

When I look at my journey with cancer, my heart attack, and now my experience with dialysis, I see how God has used each of these battles to draw me closer to Him. I've come to understand that the battles we face are not meant to destroy us—they are meant to refine us, to strengthen our faith, and to prepare us for the next level of our journey. And when we come out on the other side, we must give God the glory. We must rejoice because we know that it was His grace that sustained us, His power that delivered us, and His love that carried us through.

I often think of Paul and Silas in Acts 16. After being beaten and thrown into prison, they didn't sit there in despair. Instead, they began to sing praises to God. And as they praised, the prison doors were opened, and they were set free. Their praise didn't just change their situation—it changed the atmosphere around them. That's what praise does. It shifts the atmosphere. It changes our perspective. It reminds us that we are not defeated, but victorious in Christ.

I've seen the power of praise in my own life. After my heart attack, I was weak and unsure of how long it would take to recover fully. But I made a decision to praise God every day, even when I didn't feel like it. And as I praised Him, my strength began to return. My spirit was lifted, and I felt the joy of the Lord filling my heart. Nehemiah 8:10 says, *"For the joy of the Lord is your strength."* That joy is what kept me going, even on the hardest days.

There is something about rejoicing after the battle that brings healing to our souls. It's a reminder that God has not forgotten us, that He is still with us, and that He will continue to walk beside us in every step of our journey. Rejoicing is not just a response to victory—it's a way of proclaiming that God's promises are true, that His love is unwavering, and that His grace is sufficient for every challenge we face.

Even in my most difficult moments, I learned that rejoicing in God opens the door to deeper healing. It's like a balm for the spirit. When we rejoice, we allow God's presence to wash over us, to renew our hope, and to remind us that our lives are securely held in His hands. I believe that true joy—joy that lasts—is rooted in knowing that no matter what, God is good. He doesn't change, and neither do His promises. This kind of joy keeps us grounded and gives us the strength to keep moving forward, even when we're unsure of what lies ahead.

The journey of life is filled with hills and valleys, victories and setbacks. It's easy to praise God when we're on the mountaintop, but the real depth of our faith is revealed in how we respond after we've walked through the valley. Do we choose to dwell on the hardship, or do we lift our eyes to the One who brought us through it? For me, choosing to rejoice after each battle is my way of honoring God's faithfulness and keeping my heart aligned with His.

I remember how, even in the most challenging parts of my treatment and recovery, I found myself in awe of God's kindness. Every day He provided little glimpses of His love and care, whether through the encouragement of a friend, a prayer from a church member, or a simple moment of peace. These were reminders that God was intimately involved in every detail of my journey, that He hadn't left me for a moment. And now, as I reflect on those times, I rejoice all the more, knowing that each of those moments was a part of His greater plan for my healing and growth.

Rejoicing doesn't mean ignoring the reality of our struggles. It means choosing to acknowledge God's sovereignty in the midst of them. It means thanking Him not only for bringing us through the battles but for the strength and wisdom He's given us because of them. Each time we rejoice, we are declaring that God is greater than any obstacle we face, that His love has conquered every fear, and that His light shines brighter than the darkest night.

As I continue to walk my path, now with the added challenge of dialysis, I hold tightly to the lessons I've learned about rejoicing after the battle. I know there will be more difficulties ahead, but I am certain that God's grace will sustain me through each one. The road may not always be easy, but with God by my side, I know I am never alone. And each time I overcome an obstacle, I will continue to lift my hands in praise, giving Him the glory for every victory.

To anyone reading this who is going through their own battle, I want to encourage you: don't wait until the storm is over to find joy. Look for God's hand in the midst of it. Trust that He is working on your behalf, even when you can't see it. And when you do come through to the other side, rejoice with all your heart, knowing that the God who brought you through is the same God who will walk with you into every new season of life.

God has shown me, time and again, that we can overcome the odds. We may face what seems impossible, but nothing is impossible with Him. He is the God of miracles, the God of redemption, and the God of endless love. No matter what challenges lie ahead, I am convinced that I will keep rejoicing, for my life is a testament to His grace, His mercy, and His power to bring victory out of every battle.

CHAPTER 9

Encouragement for the Road Ahead

I encourage you to trust God through all of life's challenges. Life is full of unexpected turns, difficult trials, and sometimes overwhelming obstacles, but one thing I've learned through my journey is that God is always with us. No matter how dark the path ahead may seem, He is guiding us, strengthening us, and giving us what we need to persevere. Trusting God doesn't mean that we will always have all the answers or that we will always understand why things happen the way they do. It means believing that He is sovereign and that His plans for us are always good.

One of the most important things we can do when facing the challenges of life is to remind ourselves of who God is. He is our refuge, our strength, and our very present help in trouble (Psalm 46:1). When we are overwhelmed, He is our peace. When we are weak, He is our strength. When we are lost, He is our guide. No matter what we are going through, we can trust that God is with us, and He will never leave us or forsake us.

As you journey through life, I encourage you to hold on to this truth: God is faithful. He has been faithful in the past, He is faithful today, and He will continue to be faithful in the future. Sometimes, when we're in the middle of a storm, it's hard to see how things will work out. But as we continue to trust God and lean on His promises, we will see His hand at work in ways we never imagined.

Hold On to Hope

One of the greatest gifts God gives us is hope. No matter what we are facing, we can have hope because we know that God is in control. Hope is not based on our circumstances; it's based on who God is. Romans 5:3-5 tells us, *"And not only so, but we glory in tribulations also: knowing that tribulation worketh patience; And patience, experience; and experience, hope: And hope maketh not ashamed; because the love of God is shed abroad in our hearts by the Holy Ghost which is given unto us."*

In my own life, there have been times when I've felt like giving up. The battles with cancer, heart disease, and now dialysis have tested my faith in ways I never expected. But even in my darkest moments, I held on to hope. I believed that God had a plan for my life, and I trusted that He would bring me through. And He did. He has brought me through every trial, every hardship, and every obstacle, and I know that He will continue to carry me forward.

Hope is powerful because it gives us something to look forward to. It reminds us that no matter what we are going through today, there is a future that God is preparing for us. Jeremiah 29:11 says, *"For I know the thoughts that I think toward you, saith the Lord, thoughts of peace, and not of evil, to give you an expected end."* This scripture has been a lifeline for me during my trials, reminding me that God's plans are always good, even when I can't see the full picture.

Lean on Your Faith Community

Another important piece of advice I would offer is to lean on your faith community. We were never meant to walk through life alone. God created us to live in community with one another, to support each other, pray for each other, and encourage each other. When we face challenges, having a strong support system can make all the difference. During my battles with illness, I was uplifted by the prayers and support of my church family, the pastors of the Baptist General State Convention of Illinois, and so many friends and loved ones.

Ecclesiastes 4:9-10 tells us, *"Two are better than one; because they have a good reward for their labour. For if they fall, the one will lift up his fellow: but woe to him that is alone when he falleth; for he hath not another to help him up."* We need each other. There is strength in numbers, and when we come together as the body of Christ, we are able to carry each other through the trials of life. If you are going through a difficult season, don't hesitate to reach out to those around you. Let them pray for you, encourage you, and walk with you through the storm.

I've learned that it's okay to ask for help. Sometimes, we feel like we have to be strong all the time, but the truth is, we all need support at different times in our lives. Letting others in doesn't mean you're weak; it means you're wise. It means you recognize the value of community and the strength that comes from standing together.

Trust God's Timing

One of the most challenging things about going through trials is waiting for God's timing. We want things to happen right away, but God's timing is often different from ours. Learning to trust God's timing is a crucial part of the faith journey. Isaiah 40:31 says, *"But they that wait upon the Lord shall renew their strength; they shall mount up with wings as eagles; they shall run, and not be weary; and they shall walk, and not faint."* This verse reminds us that when we wait on the Lord, He renews our strength.

There have been many times in my life when I've had to wait on God's timing. When I was diagnosed with cancer, I had to wait for treatment to work. When I had my heart attack, I had to wait for my body to heal. And now, as I'm on dialysis, I'm waiting for a kidney transplant. Waiting is not easy, but I've learned that God is working in the waiting. He is shaping us, refining us, and preparing us for what's ahead. His timing is always perfect, even when we don't understand it.

If you're in a season of waiting, I encourage you to trust God. Don't give up. Keep praying, keep believing, and keep trusting that God is working behind the scenes. Sometimes, the greatest growth happens in the waiting. God uses these times to strengthen our faith and teach us to rely on Him more fully.

Keep Moving Forward

No matter what challenges you face, I encourage you to keep moving forward. Don't let the trials of life keep you stuck. Keep pressing on, keep trusting God, and keep believing that He has a plan for your life. Philippians 3:13-14 says, *"Brethren, I count not myself to have apprehended: but this one thing I do, forgetting those things which are behind, and reaching forth unto those things which are before, I press toward the mark for the prize of the high calling of God in Christ Jesus."* This scripture is a reminder to keep our eyes on the future and not get bogged down by the challenges of the past.

There will be times when you feel like you can't go on, but I want to remind you that with God's strength, you can. God has given you everything you need to persevere. He has equipped you with His Word, His Spirit, and His grace. And He promises to be with you every step of the way.

Encouragement from Scripture

As you face life's challenges, I encourage you to immerse yourself in the Word of God. The Bible is filled with promises of hope, strength, and encouragement for every situation we face. Here are a few scriptures that have encouraged me along the way, and I pray they will encourage you too:

Psalm 34:17-19: *"The righteous cry, and the Lord heareth, and delivereth them out of all their troubles. The Lord is nigh unto them that are of a broken heart; and saveth such as be of a contrite spirit. Many are the afflictions of the righteous: but the Lord delivereth him out of them all."*

Isaiah 41:10: *"Fear thou not; for I am with thee: be not dismayed; for I am thy God: I will strengthen thee; yea, I* will help thee; yea, I will uphold thee with the right hand of my righteousness."

2 Corinthians 4:8-9: *"We are troubled on every side, yet not distressed; we are perplexed, but not in despair; Persecuted, but not forsaken; cast down, but not destroyed."*

Proverbs 3:5-6: *"Trust in the Lord with all thine heart; and lean not unto thine own understanding. In all thy ways acknowledge him, and he shall direct thy paths."*

These scriptures remind us that no matter what we are facing, God is with us. He is our refuge, our strength, and our guide. As we trust in Him, He will lead us through every trial and give us the strength to keep moving forward.

Final Encouragement: Overcoming the Odds

As I reflect on my journey, one truth stands clear: with God, we can overcome the odds. Life's challenges may seem insurmountable at times, but I am living proof that no obstacle is too great for our God. Whether facing illness, loss, or uncertainty, we serve a God who specializes in turning what seems impossible into victory.

I encourage you to remember that God has a purpose for each of us, and His plans are filled with hope and a future, no matter what hardships we encounter. Sometimes, our struggles can seem to overshadow our purpose, but the truth is that our greatest growth often emerges from our greatest trials. Every obstacle we overcome strengthens our faith and deepens our relationship with God. It allows us to testify to His goodness, not only for ourselves but for everyone who hears our story.

When I faced cancer, heart disease, and even my journey with dialysis, there were times I didn't understand why I had to go through such pain. But now, looking back at all of it, I can see how each struggle played a role in shaping me and strengthening my faith. God used those battles to reveal His power and to show me, and those around me, that with Him, all things are possible.

Overcoming the odds is not simply about emerging from difficulty—it's about rising with a deeper understanding of God's presence in our lives. It's about knowing that God's love carries us through every high and low, and that He will never leave us nor forsake us. I've come to realize that when we face overwhelming odds, we have an opportunity to demonstrate our faith and trust in ways that speak louder than words.

When we hold on to hope, lean on our community, trust God's timing, and keep moving forward, we display a faith that stands strong despite the storms. This kind of faith doesn't just impact our lives; it impacts the lives of those who witness our journey. People are drawn to a life that overcomes, a life that reflects the power of God at work within us. Our trials become testimonies, and our stories of overcoming encourage others to trust God in their own battles.

So, as you continue on the road ahead, remember that with God, nothing is impossible. When challenges arise, and when you feel the weight of the world on your shoulders, take a moment to reflect on God's promises. Let His Word remind you that you are not alone and that He is fighting for you. Isaiah 41:13 says, *"For I the Lord thy God will hold thy right hand, saying unto thee, Fear not; I will help thee."* This assurance is a reminder that we do not face life's battles in our own strength but with the mighty hand of God guiding and sustaining us.

Each day is an opportunity to overcome, to stand firm in our faith, and to show the world what it means to trust God fully. And as you press on, know that every step you take, no matter how small, is a step closer to victory. With each challenge you overcome, your faith will grow stronger, your purpose clearer, and your spirit renewed. The road may not always be easy, but the rewards of faith, perseverance, and trust in God are beyond measure.

As you look forward, my prayer is that you would find strength in knowing that God has equipped you for this journey. He has placed within you everything you need to overcome the odds, to rise above every trial, and to live a life that reflects His goodness and faithfulness. Hold on to His promises, lean on those He has placed in your life, and never lose sight of the hope that is found in Him. God is with you, and with Him, you can overcome anything.

About the Author

Dr. Mark A. McConnell was born on February 7, 1963, and raised in Kansas City, Kansas, by devoted Christian parents. From a young age, his faith was central to his life, accepting Christ at the tender age of five. Dr. McConnell's foundational  spiritual upbringing was nurtured at Mt. Zion Baptist Church under the guidance of Dr. C.L. Bachus.

He pursued higher education with a commitment to his calling, earning a Bachelor's degree in Religion and Philosophy from Bishop College in Dallas, Texas, in 1986. He continued his theological education, receiving a Master of Divinity from Midwestern Baptist Theological Seminary in Kansas City, Missouri, in 1989 and completing a Doctor of Theology (Th.D.) in May 2002.

Dr. McConnell has been blessed with a beautiful family. He married Paris McConnell, his steadfast partner and source of strength, on September 2, 1989. Together, they have three sons—Moses, Caleb, and Matthew—and are proud grandparents to Jayden and Jordan McConnell.

Answering the call to preach, Dr. McConnell delivered his first sermon in May 1984 and was ordained in August 1985. His pastoral journey has included leading three congregations: Southside First Baptist Church in Kansas City, Missouri; Prince of Peace Baptist Church in Peoria, Illinois; and currently, New Cornerstone Baptist Church in Peoria, Illinois. His service extends beyond the pulpit, having served two terms as Moderator of the Central Illinois Baptist District Association in Peoria, Illinois. His involvement with the Baptist General State Convention of Illinois spans over 31 years, during which he has held significant positions, including 2nd Vice President of both the Baptist General Congress of Christian Education and the Baptist General State Convention of Illinois.

Dr. McConnell's dedication and unwavering commitment have led to his current role as President of the Baptist General State Convention of Illinois. His passion for this esteemed body is evident in his consistent participation, having never missed a board meeting, annual session, or Congress of Christian Education. He firmly believes that God has positioned him to lead and serve, fostering unity and growth within the convention.

Dr. McConnell's vision is clear: to uphold and advance the legacy of the Baptist General State Convention of Illinois, continuing its history as a leading force among state conventions. Through dedication and collective effort, he is confident that this convention will remain a beacon of leadership, faith, and service.

Printed in the United States
by Baker & Taylor Publisher Services